INSTAGRAM SECRETS (VOL.1)

How to find the right
INSTAGRAM AUDIENCE

Become an Influencer and build a
Business with no money on Instagram

Short social media marketing book

By **Rossitza Toneva**

First edition

☐

Table of content

The three major ways to make money with Instagram?

You have in your hands the first volume of twelve pieces puzzle named "Instagram Secrets". This puzzle includes the following pieces:

HOW to find the right Instagram AUDIENCE?
HOW to Build the Perfect Instagram PROFILE?
HOW to create Instagram KILLER CONTENTS?
HOW to outsmart Instagram ALGORITHM?
HOW to use Instagram HASHTAGS?
HOW to use Instagram METRICS?
HOW to use Instagram DIRECT MESSAGING?
HOW to use Instagram IGTV content?
HOW to use Instagram CONTESTS?
HOW to use Instagram INFLUENCERS?
HOW to use Instagram AUTOMATION TOOLS?
How to generate PROFITS from Instagram?

Each element above contributes to growing your Instagram account. You must understand the secrets of all twelve pieces. That's why I created a set of 12 books. Thanks to this step- by –step set of books, you are going to learn a lot of tricks that nobody shares with you.

Instagram is the main social media platform, with over a billion monthly users, 71% of whom are under 35. So if you want to build a business and your target is millennials, Instagram is the right communication platform.

Keep in mind that there are three major ways to make money on Instagram.

- Work as an influencer to post content sponsored by brands.
- Be an affiliate marketer selling other people's products.

- Become or be an entrepreneur and sell your products or service.

You can learn more about these specific topics in the last book of the collection: **Instagram Secrets Vol 12: How to generate PROFITS from Instagram. Become an influencer and build a business with no money on Instagram.**

So keep reading all twelve books.

You can find the entire books collection on the next pages:

These are the first 6 books of the collection. Thanks to these first books you are going to learn the basic Instagram tools: AUDIENCE; PROFILE; KILLER CONTENTS ALGORITHM; HASHTAGS; METRICS.

The next image contains the other six books: DIRECT MESSAGING; IGTV CONTENT; CONTEST; INFLUENCERS; AUTOMATION TOOLS; PROFITS.

So once you read through, this set of 12 books I am convinced you are going to become a real Instagram expert. Make sure that you read and understand each book before you move to the next one. You will quickly see that all book strategies are connected. Only when you get the whole picture you can fully understand how to create your Winning Instagram strategy.

Think that thanks to Instagram you could turn your passions into money and build a business, but before you must know all the Powerful Secrets.

Growing your Instagram following requires consistent commitment and dedication. You will not get the results you are looking for if you are not working and build your Instagram page every single day. So you need to think about:

What you are looking to get out of Instagram?

Why are you making an Instagram account?

What kind of goals do you want to achieve with your Instagram account: follower growth, brand awareness, or just revenue?

All my short step by step guides have a section, named **Homework task**. So take your time to write down your ideas. I am going to help you to clarify your thoughts guiding you step by step. The Homework section is going to be split into 4 sections:

An influencer with no Instagram profile or existing Instagram profile with less than 100 followers;

An influencer with an already existing Instagram profile and over 100 followers;

Small business with no Instagram profile or existing Instagram profile with less than 100 followers;

Small business with already existing Instagram profile and over 100 followers;

The homework section is really important because it offers you the opportunity to understand what to do in this first stage of the work. Try to experiment with all the ideas that you write down in the Homework section, using your Instagram profile. When you write down your ideas you automatically focus your full attention on them. Remember that you have to experiment.

Before we start I would like to give you a special bonus - the opportunity to get one of my books for free. Send me an email at rtineva80@gmail.com. Please indicate the name of the book that you bought and the day. Send me the name of the new book as well.

Please do not forget, if you enjoyed this book and found some benefit in reading it, to post a review on Amazon. Your feedback and support will help me to greatly improve my writing craft for future projects. And make this book even better.

In this specific short guide, I'll discuss in-depth tactics and strategies on how to define your own Instagram audience coherently with your earning strategy.

Remember that you can contact me for one to one Skype session as well.

Let's get started.

Why you should read this book?

This book is for all Instagram users that are interested in Organic (No payment) Instagram Growth of their account, investing only their time and little amount of money. That means you don't buy fake followers, use farmed accounts to build your following, invest money in agencies, or expansive campaigns. You get FREE Instagram followers thanks to your effort and work.

If you want to attract real people who are interested in your content, you should learn how to work on the organic growth for your Instagram account and how to earn money through Instagram.

Having in-depth knowledge of your Instagram target audience is an essential part of a successful social media strategy.

Unless you know what intrigues and motivates your followers, you'll have a hard time producing the right content to engage them. And unless you know when they are active, you won't have much success reaching them at the right time.

So, you must learn how to find your target audience on Instagram and discover the best targeting tactics to reach them. This book is going to help you do exactly that. Do not forget to consult the last chapter named Homework. This chapter is very useful to explain better some of the concepts of this book.

If you have some problem with the terminology used, consult the last chapter of this book, named: "Common Instagram terms you should know"?

Introduction

Think about Instagram as an instrument that can help you to sell something and to earn money. If you want to grow your followers you have to work hard, and you have to know why you make this effort. So the first thing to do is think about the aim of your Instagram growing project.

Many people make the mistake of desiring to become Influencer without thinking about why they are going to invest their time in growing their Instagram account.

Thanks to this book you can learn some of the most important Marketing tips on how to find the right Instagram Audience and start to grow slowly your account.

You are going to learn the difference between the Target market and Target audience as well. And how to be sure that the audience you choose is the right one for your product or service?

In the modern, digital world, we're constantly bombarded with huge amounts of information. If you're not out there speaking to a specific group of people, there's a good chance your message will end up drowning in that sea of unfocused noise.

Having many followers is undoubtedly something you should aspire to, but you have to worry if none of them show any interest in the content that you post. To convert your Instagram followers into customers or people interested in your profile, you need to focus on the right people and to create your target audience according to the product or service that want to offer. Everything has to be coherent and aligned: product, message, and audience.

Think about the following quote: *"If you try to sell to everyone, then you'll end up selling to No-one."*

Chapter 1: How to define your Target Market?

Remember that your first aim is to think about **what I can sell through Instagram**? So defining your target market is one of the marketer's most important tasks. It's the foundation of all elements of your marketing strategy. How you develop and name your products? What kind of marketing channels you will use to promote your services or products?

A target market refers to a group of potential customers who are going to use your product or service.

Identifying the target market is an essential step for you in the development of a marketing plan. Not knowing who the target market is could cost a lot of money and time for you.

Try to correctly identify customers' needs not satisfied before you define your typical customer looks like.

The target market typically consists of consumers who exhibit similar characteristics (such as age, location, income, or lifestyle) and are considered most likely to buy the same product or service.

Social media platforms, such as Facebook, LinkedIn, Twitter, and Instagram, have sophisticated options to allow businesses to target users based on market segments. For that reason, Instagram and Facebook are very useful instruments and you can use them for your communication campaign.

Let's take a real example that you want to create a Luxury Travel blog.

Before you start to set up your marketing strategy, try to ask yourself the following questions:

What are the needs and problems that I'll satisfy with my product or service?
Answer: No web site describes and compares the benefits of luxury hotels around the world.

Identifying the needs, expectations, and problems of your target not only helps you to understand them better, but it also ensures that you're creating a product or service that's going to have a real impact on the marketplace.

Think about what problems your target customers face in day-to-day life, and how your product could solve those issues.

What kind of product or service I can offer?

Answer: I want to create an information blog, specializes to promote luxury hotels all over the world.

What is my final aim?

Answer: I want to earn money from affiliate marketing, direct sponsorship, and advertising. (*Affiliate marketing is the process by which an affiliate earns a commission for marketing another person's or company's products. The affiliate simply searches for a product they enjoy, then promotes that product and earns a piece of the profit from each sale they make*).

What audience do I want to attract?

Answer: People that love to travel with financial resources to afford luxury hotels.

What is my target looking for (demographic description)?

Answer: Men and Women, 25 – 70 age, a high-level target that lives in Europe and the USA.

A "target persona" is simply a description of your ideal customer, using details such as:

Age
Gender
Children
Income
Occupation
Geographic location
Hobbies
Goals
Challenges

You should create a potential "target persona" for your brand. In simple terms, a target persona is a profile of an ideal customer that you want to use your product.

To create your potential "target persona", you need to take a closer look at the products or services you offer and think of the people they are best suited for. I would like to give you another example.

For instance, assuming you're selling men's luxury watches with art design and a high price tag. In that case, your target persona is a man who likes to wear watches, who has the financial resources to afford a luxury timepiece, and loves art. That is the type of person you would want to have as your loyal customer.

There are so many factors you can incorporate when you're discovering how to identify a target market. The more you understand the wants, goals, and challenges of your customers, the easier it will be to design a campaign that grabs their attention.

In the next chapter, you can learn how you can start to design your buyer persona.

Chapter 2: How to define your Buyer Personas?

In this chapter, I would like to go deeper and to explain the difference between a Target Market and a Buyer Personas.

Think of it in this way: your **target market** is the group of people who could benefit from your product or service. ***The buyer personas are the people you're selling to.***

Take this example, children's books. The **target market** is kids aged 4 to 10, but the **buyer personas** include parents and grandparents of young children, libraries, elementary schools, and teachers.

Target marketing aims to connect with a group of consumers most likely to purchase what you have to offer based on demographics, past buying history, and other data.

Being specific is also relevant to marketing. **Many new business owners or entrepreneurs make the mistake of thinking that their product or service is great for everybody, but that's just not so.**

I would like to show how to conduct **buyer personas research** in five simple steps.

Step 1: To whom I can sell my product?

Think again about geo-demographic characteristics. This time the focus will be who can buy my products?

If we think about our previous example Children's book. You can get different customer potential profiles:

Profile 1: Parents, from 25 to 45 ages.

Profile 2: Grandparents from 50 to 80 ages.

Target market and buyer personas groups have a lot of overlap, and in many cases, they may be the same for your business.

Step 2: Create clear communication messages about the value of your product or service.

All marketers must understand the **difference between features and benefits**. You can list the features of your product/service all day long, but no one will be convinced to buy from you unless you can explain the benefits.

Features are what your product is or does. The benefits are the results. Essentially, benefits can be thought of as the primary reason a customer would choose to buy whatever you're selling.

How does your product make someone's life easier, or better, or just more interesting?

For example, IKEA features of the advertised furniture might be that it is small, inexpensive, and multi-purpose. **But the benefit is that it can help you make a small, temporary living space feel like home.**

Based on the identified needs, expectations, and problems of your target audience you can create effective promotion messages for each buyer profile that you identified in step 1.

Step 3: Profile of existing customers.

The easiest way to know your target audience is to examine your existing clients.

So a great first step in figuring out who most wants to buy from you is to identify who is already using your products or services.

Even if you only have a couple of customers right now, it's worth speaking to them and finding out what they have in common. Loyal repeat customers can help you to understand what kind of people you should be targeting with your brand and products. Once you understand the defining characteristics of your existing customer base, you can go after more people who fit the same mold.

If you do not have existing clients skip directly to the next paragraph: Step 4: Check out the competition.

Depending on how someone connects with your business, you might have only a little information about them or a lot.

But whatever information you do have about your existing customers into a database you can use to track trends and averages. Some data points you might want to consider are:

Age: You don't need to get too specific here. But knowing which decade of life your customers are in, or their generation can be very useful.

Location: (and time zone): Where in the world do your existing customers live? In addition to understanding which geographic areas to target, this helps you figure out what hours are most important for your customer service and sales reps to be online, and when you should schedule your social ads and posts to ensure the best visibility.

Language: Don't assume your customers speak the same language you do. And don't assume they speak the dominant language of their (or your) current physical location.

Spending power and patterns: How much money do your current customers have to spend? How do they approach purchases in your price category? Do they have specific financial concerns or preferences you need to address?

Interests: What do your customers like to do, besides using your products or services? What TV shows do they watch? What other businesses do they interact with?

Stage of life: Are your customers likely to be college students? New parents? Parents of teens? Retirees?

Step 4: Check out the competition.

Now that you know who's already interacting with your account or business and buying your products or services, it's time to see who's engaging with the competition.

Taking a look at what your competitors are up to can help you answer some key questions: Are your competitors going after the same market segments as you are? Are they reaching segments you hadn't thought to consider? How are they positioning themselves? What kind of communication instruments your competitors use?

You won't be able to get detailed audience research about the people interacting with your competitors, but you'll be able to get a general sense of the approach they're taking and whether it's allowing them to create engagement online. This analysis will help you understand which markets they're targeting and whether their efforts appear to be effective.

Step 5: How am I going to attract my target audience?

What kind of communication instruments I'll use?

I am going to create a Word press page, Facebook page, Instagram account or invest in Google ads.

Can I use Instagram to reach my target audience? If your answer is yes, go ahead with the next chapter.

☐

Chapter 3: Do Instagram is the right communication tool for your Target Audience?

Defining your **target audience** gives you a solid foundation to understand if your potential customers use social media and what kind of social media they use.

You need to find out who your social media target audience is and go there to market to them.

I would like to summarize the three main topics of the first chapters with the table below:

	Target Market	Buyer Personas	Instagram Target Audience
DEFINITION	Target market is the group of people who could benefit from your product or service.	The target audience are the people you're selling to.	Instagram target audience is one of the instruments that you can use to reach your audience. You can use Facebook, Google, Snapchat, Tic Tok as well.
	Target Person	Target Audience Person	Instagram Target persona
WITH ONE WORD	TARGET	BUY	COMUNICATE
QUESTIONS	Who could benefit from your product or service?	Who could purchase your product and service?	How and what I am going to communicate to my potential customers?
EXAMPLE	Take this example, a luxury set of sheets.		
	The target market is a person who appreciates luxury products and have financial resources.	Target audience could include hotels, final consumers, who want to make a nice present.	You can use Instagram to find accounts that advertise or speak about Luxury products.

Remember that the Target market and Buyer personas groups have a lot of overlap.

I would like to give you some data about who is using the most important social media today. This information is very important to decide what kind of communication channel you are going to choose for your social campaigns and target audience.

Facebook Audience Statistics 2019.

Facebook audience research shows it's still the most frequently used social media platform, with 2.23 billion people log in to the platform every month. Based on the total population, (not just internet users) a full 30% of the **Facebook ad audience, is aged 25 through 34.** According to "We Are Social", America is the second-biggest population on Facebook having around 270 million users. Because of that, it's a safe bet that your brand or your client's brand will be on Facebook — all you need is to target them in the right way. I would like to share with you some survey figures prepared by Statista.

Distribution of Facebook users worldwide as of October 2019, by age and gender

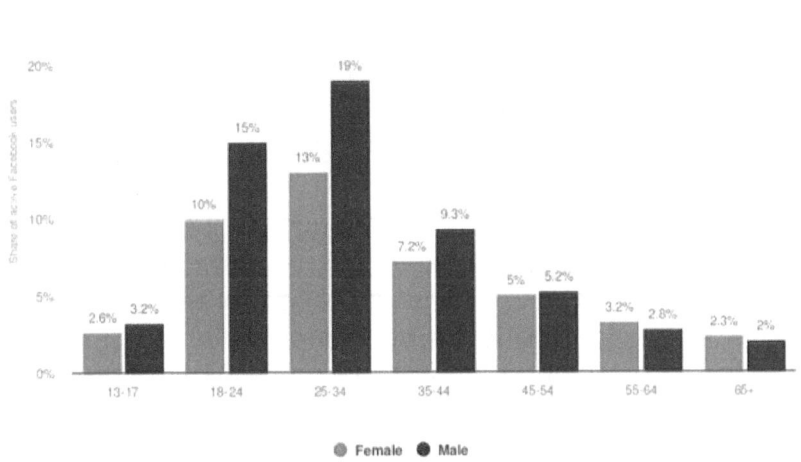

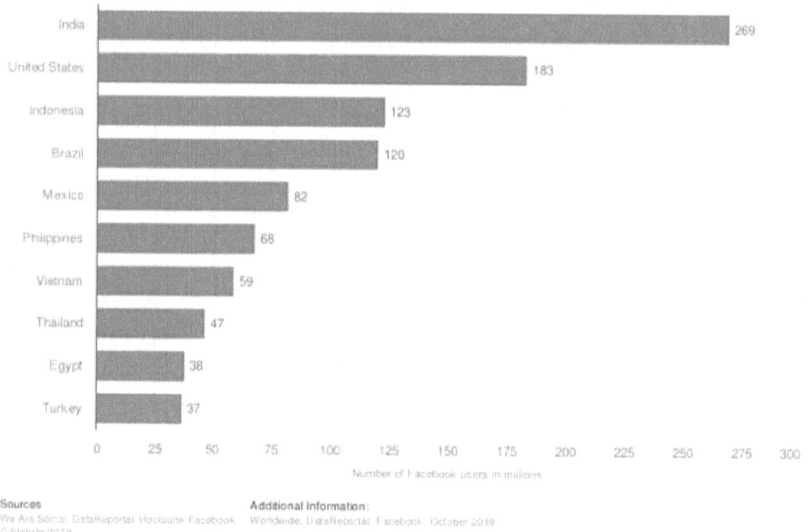

Leading countries based on number of Facebook users as of October 2019 (in millions)

Country	Users
India	269
United States	183
Indonesia	123
Brazil	120
Mexico	82
Philippines	68
Vietnam	59
Thailand	47
Egypt	38
Turkey	37

Number of Facebook users in millions

Sources
We Are Social, DataReportal, Hootsuite, Facebook, © Statista 2019

Additional Information:
Worldwide, DataReportal, Facebook, October 2019

So in case, you would like to communicate with man customers from the USA or India with 25 – 35 years, probably the best social tool is Facebook.

Twitter Audience Statistics 2019.

According to Cision, 326 million people use Twitter every month.

Statistics also say that 37% of Twitter users are between the ages **of 18 and 25 years** while 25% of users are 30-49 years old. That means, younger Americans are more likely to be on Twitter than older Americans. When you're planning your social media calendar and you have a heavy Twitter user ratio, make sure you create some compelling Tweets — the ones which will be interesting for an audience of this age.

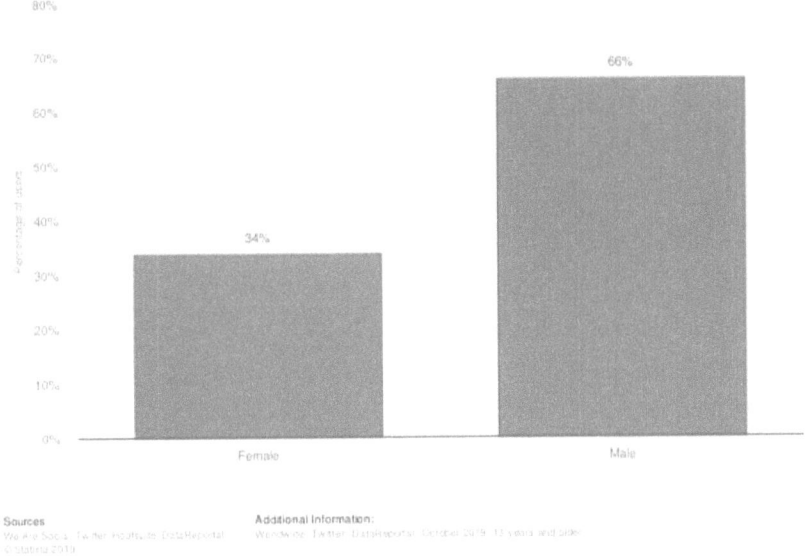

Distribution of Twitter users worldwide as of October 2019, by gender

So if you want to communicate with the male gander between (18-25 age) the best social tool to use is Twitter.

Instagram Audience Statistics 2019.

It's already 1 billion monthly active Instagram users, Omnicore shows. Interesting fact: women more than men use this photo-sharing app, and being perfectly precise it's 39% of women and 30% of men. However, there are plenty of millennials on the platform, so if you have people in that age range (under 49), who are a part of your demographic target, it makes sense to find your audience on Instagram. You can find further information about Instagram usage in the graphic on the next page.

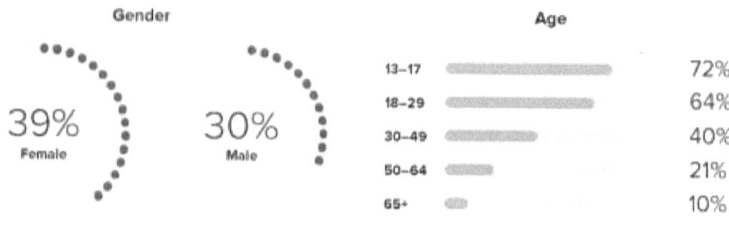

Instagram usage among key demographics

Gender

39%
Female

30%
Male

Age

13–17		72%
18–29		64%
30–49		40%
50–64		21%
65+		10%

Location

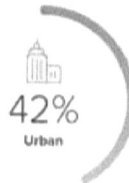

42%
Urban

34%
Suburban

25%
Rural

Income

30% 42% 32% 42%

< $30K

$30K–$49,999

$30K–$74,999

$75K +

Education

High school degree or less	29%
Some college	36%
College+	42%

sproutsocial   http://www.pewinternet.org/2018/03/01/social-media-use-in-2018/

The graphic shows that promote your product through social media like Instagram make sense if your target audience includes people aged under 49 years. **The typical profile of the person that uses Instagram is: woman, from 13 to 49 years, lives in an urban location with a college degree and high incomes from 30k to 49 k dollars or more than 75k dollars.**

The next chapters will help you to develop better your Instagram idea.

Once you have defined better your Instagram target you can create your Instagram profile, for further information and tips check my book: Instagram Secrets Vol 2: HOW to Build the Perfect Instagram Profile. Become an influencer and build a business with no money on Instagram.

Chapter 4: How to Use the Instagram search bar to find useful information that can help you to find your Target audience?

Instagram is one of the few social media platforms with a Search and Explore tab in its app.

There are several ways you can use Instagram's Search or Explore Page for your business - finding competitors, the best hashtags to use, engaging your fans, and finding influencers to collaborate with.

Let's first understand what you can search and explore on Instagram.

1. Open your Instagram app.
2. Tap the ***magnifying glass icon*** to go to the Search and Explore tab.

3. Try to tap some keyword in the "search bar". The keyword has to be related to your product /service let's say *"Travel"*.

4. Now you can find 4 sections: **Top, Accounts, Tags, and Places**. I would like to explain better how these four sections work.

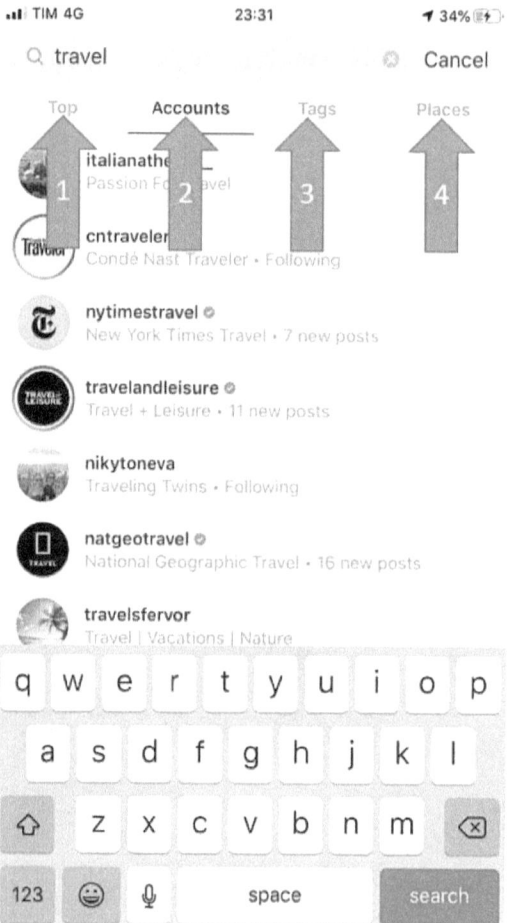

You can search for the following:

Top section: Essentially the 'Top accounts' on Instagram are picked out by an algorithm that attempts to rank accounts strongly related to the word "travel", that could be to your interest because you follow them, or just because you checked their profile a few days ago.

Accounts section: Essentially you can find people or other Instagram users. All the accounts in this section have the keyword "**travel**" in their Username or Name.

Remember to add "@" before your keywords when you are searching for people in the Action section.

Tags section: you can check all the hashtags that use the word "Travel" in their name. You can check how many posts each hashtag has inside. So you can check the popularity of one hashtag.
You can find the instagramers that used the hashtag "Travel" in their post as well.
Remember to add "#" before your keywords when you are searching for hashtags.

Places: you can find Location tags and to check the places next to you that used "Travel" in their username. It could be events or locations as well.

Use Search bars to find competitors or potential followers.
Now I would like to show you a different type of searches:

How to find related hashtags?

When you think about the Hashtags search you have to think about the "Tags section".
It is very important to understand **how you can find the related hashtags**. This feature could help you to find more hashtags that work for your account. For example, if you know that your account works the keyword "Travel" as a hashtag you could check for related hashtags and use them in your next post to have more effective hashtags.
Instagram would suggest related hashtags near the top of the app.
For example, a travel agency's shop owner could search for hashtags "travel in Europe,"

The steps to find "Related" hashtags are the following:

Step 1: Write "Traveleurope" in the search bar and tap the "Tags" section. Instagram is going to offer you, different hashtag groups, as "traveleuope", "traveleuope2018" etc.

Step 2: Click the "Traveleurope" hashtag.

Step 3: Check the list of "Related" hashtags.

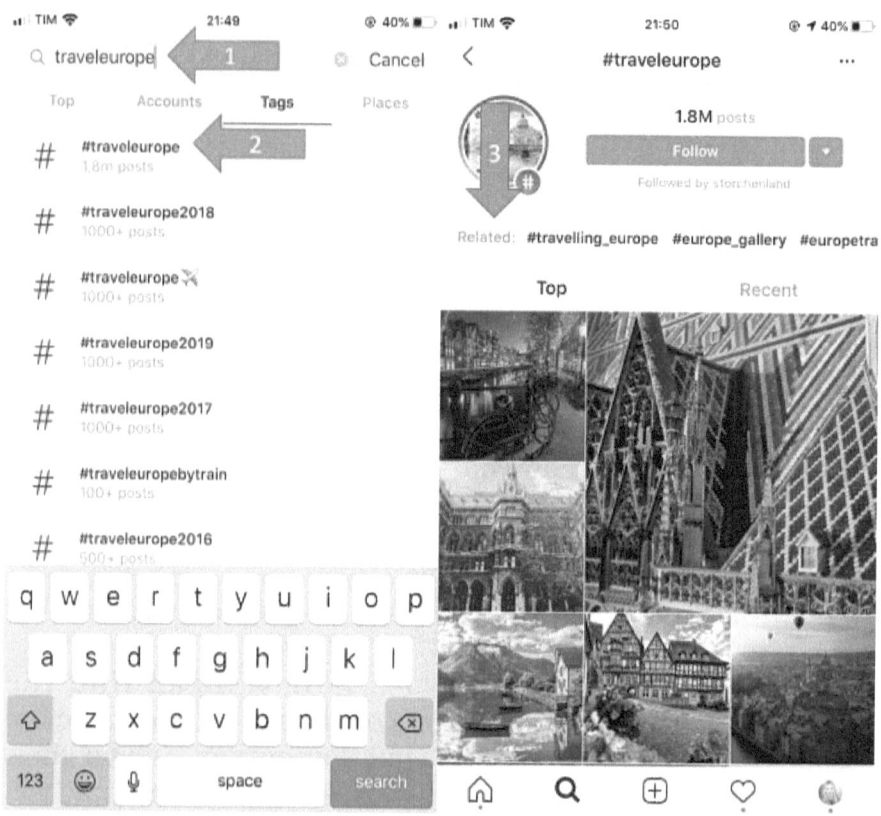

From there, you could explore the related hashtags and check out how popular the hashtag is and how frequently it is being used. Pick a few pictures that you will find in the hashtag section. See what type of content they share on their profiles. And what kind of hashtags they use.

You can use related hashtags to find your competitors as well.

How to find competitor's accounts?

When you think about Competitors you have to use the tap "Account".

Click on the "Account" category and search for profiles that use relevant keywords for their profile name and username.

For example, a travel agency in Milano city could search for "travel agency Milano" and find the following results: irantravelmilano, travel_milano, etc. Please see the picture below.

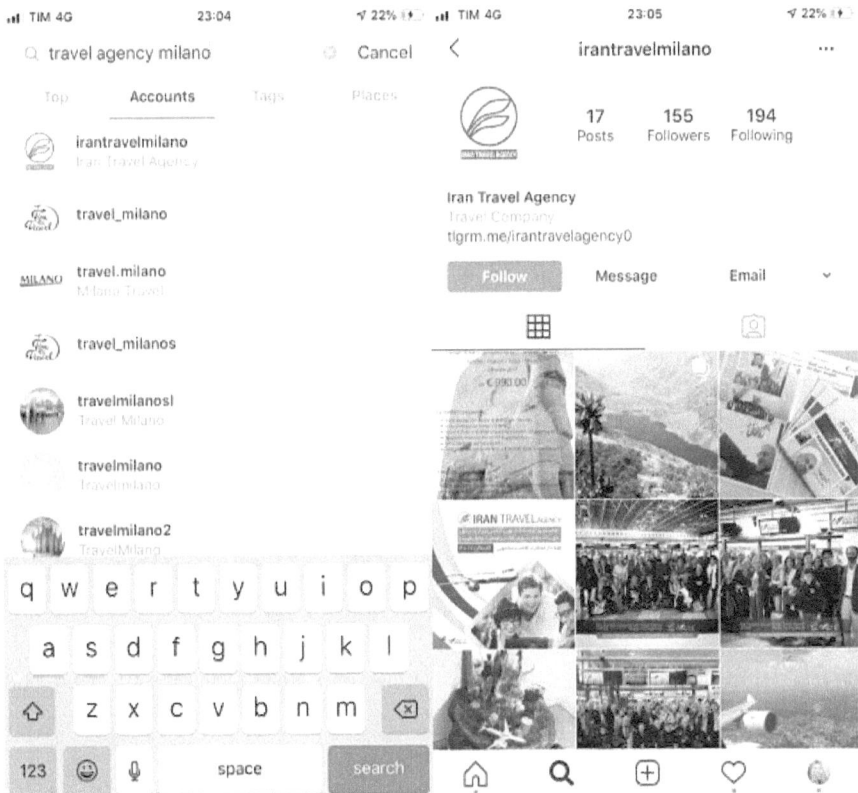

Once you have the list as indicated in the picture above, click on the accounts to see what kind of contents offer. Try to understand if the accounts could be your potential competitors.

This method is great for local businesses as well. Instagram seems to personalize your search results based on your location and the profiles you follow.

Another way is to search for relevant local business competitors is by searching through location tags.

For example, the owner of a small Milan travel agency could tab in the search bar "#travel agency Milano" and click the "Places" tab as well.

In this way, you can find all travel agencies that have an Instagram profile and are located in your catchment area. Make sure that you have location turned on for Instagram in your phone's settings. To do this, leave the Instagram app and go to the Location services section of your phone's settings.

Each time visit all the profiles that Instagram offers you and try to understand if they could be your competitors.

How to find similar accounts "Suggested by Instagram"?

When you have found a potential influencer partner and followed it, Instagram would suggest similar accounts for you to follow. If the suggestions don't appear, you can tap on the downward arrow beside "Follow" or "Following" to see the suggestions. See the example below.

The steps to find "Suggested by Instagram" accounts are the following:

Step 1: write "*Travel*" in the search bar and tap the "Account" section.

Step 2: Select one of the accounts that you see displayed, for example, "*Natgeotravel*".

Step 3: Tap "*Follow*" and you can see the "*Suggested to you*" accounts.

Step 4: Check all "Suggested *to you* "accounts.

You can see the image below to understand better step 3 and step 4.

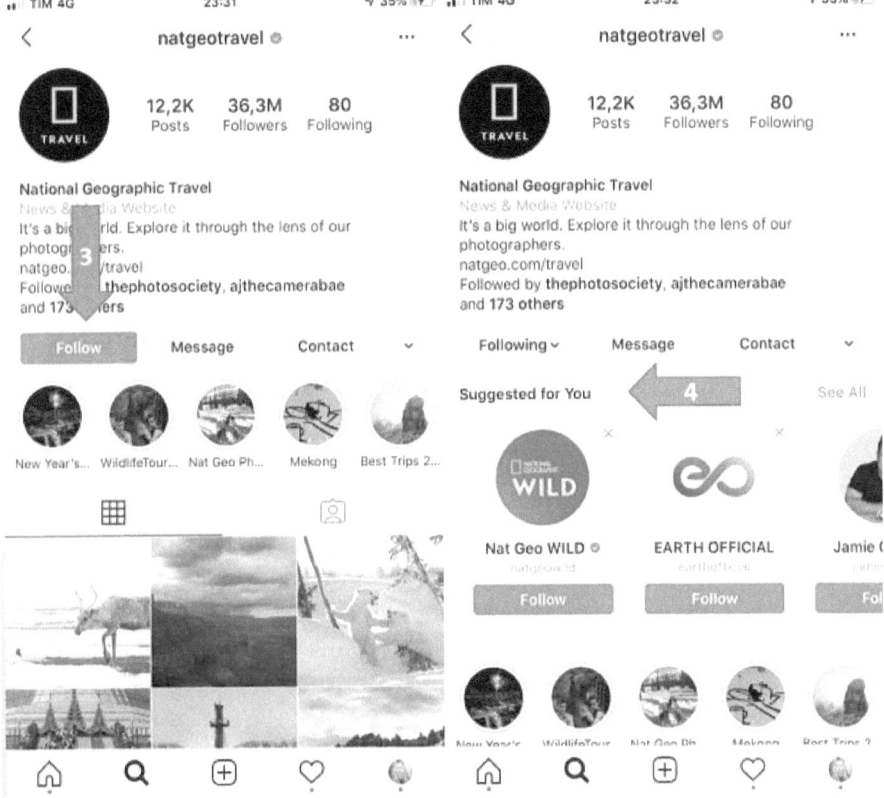

This option is important for the following two reasons.

- You can **find your direct competitors** according to the Instagram algorithm. In this case, use the mobile of your friend, and try to unfollow your profile and then to follow back it again. You can see into the section "**Suggested to your accounts**" all your direct competitors according to Instagram.

- You can **find similar accounts** for your future Instagram campaigns. For example, you know that an influencer as Leonardo di Caprio could be perfect for your next influencer campaign, but to engage him costs a lot. So try to check if Instagram could suggest you similar influencer that does not have a lot of followers and could be perfect for your Influencer campaign. Using the method illustrated above. You are going to find the account as "Conservationorg" with 484k followers that could be a perfect partner for your future campaign.

Chapter 5: Easy Three-step formula for finding your Instagram Profile niche?

The first thing to do is to evaluate **your passions and skills.** This sounds so basic, but it makes all the difference. Don't just choose a niche because you're "kind of interested" in it; to be sustainable, it should ideally be something you can see yourself being passionate about for at least 5 years.

Here are a few prompts to help you determine what your interests and passions are:

- How do you like to spend your free time? What do you look forward to doing when you aren't doing it?
- What magazines do you subscribe to? What topics do you like to learn about most?
- What clubs or organizations do you belong to?

It's also important to think about which areas you have special skills or experience in. What do people regularly tell you you're good at? What's your training or education? What special skills or knowledge have you developed through your work?

Make a list of 5 topical interests and passion areas, immediately.

With your list of 5 topics in hand, you're ready to start narrowing down your options. **To create a profitable business, you first need to find problems your target customers are experiencing, then determine whether you can solve them**. Here are several things you can do to identify problems in specific niches:

Have one-on-one conversations or idea-extraction sessions with your target market. Make sure to find or create a framework for asking questions that helps you uncover pain points.

Peruse forums to check what problems people have. Search *Quora* (www.quora.com) or find forums related to your niche, then take a look at the discussions that are taking place. What questions are people asking? What problems do they have?

Research keywords to find popular search terms for your hashtag research. Explore different keyword combinations on *Google Trends (trends.google.com)* and *Google AdWords'* keyword planner **(ads.google.com).** This can help you uncover popular search terms related to pain points.

You also want to make sure there's a need for your idea otherwise your work will stay a hobby, never growing into a lucrative business.

One way to start figuring out the market is with some basic keyword research. The *Google Keyword Planner* is a great tool for this. So try to use it as a tool as well.

Find 5 keywords related to your account idea.

1st keyword
2nd keyword
3rd keyword
4th keyword
5th keyword

Ex: Let's say I want to create something related to Travel. I can use the following keywords.

1st keyword: Travel
2nd keyword: Holiday
3rd keyword: Trip
4th keyword: Vacation
5th keyword: Hotels

After you have defined your five keywords, we are going to analyze them on Instagram.

Step 1: Tap Instagram magnifying glass;

Step 2: Write the first keyword "Travel" into the search bar.

Step3: Click on the "Tag" tab.

Step4: Check how popular the "Travel" niche on Instagram is?

Check how popular your niche in Instagram is?

Check how many posts you see in one of the Travel hashtag groups displayed by Instagram. See the image below.

For example "travelphotography" has 103 million posts inside. "traveleurope" 1.8 million. The numbers illustrate that "travel" is a really big and generic niche.

This information should help you to understand how popular one niche is. And then try to find under – segments that are not so generic. Think of something that can be unique and easily recognizable. It is better to have a small then a big general account.

Use the same method to check the other four keywords: holiday, trip, vacation, and hotel.

Let's see how to develop our idea with 3 step formula.

"3-step level down" formula for finding a niche

I will walk you through a 3-step formula for finding a niche that's both lucrative and something you can feel passionate about.

You can use the level down niche method. At minimum 2 or 3 levels down.

Take the following example, if you live in Europe, and you want to create a Travel account you can choose "TravelEurope" as a niche to pursue. But "Travel Europe" is not a specific niche enough. So what you can do is follow the method below:

Ask yourself the question "TravelEurope" for who?

Answer: Tips for Travel for Moms, so Travel in Europe for Moms with their children.

You have to think about what problem you are solving. I can create an account of how to travel in Europe with children. And to share things to do with kids traveling in Europe.

So the 3 levels deep niche is the following:
- **Level 1:** Travel
- **Level 2:** Travel in Europe
- **Level 3:** Travel in Europe with kids.

You can go one level deeper if you want:
- **Level 4**: Travel in Europe with infants (from 0 to 2 years).

I would like to give you one more example. My account RosyOnTravel has two-level niches.
Level 1: Instagram fans.
Level 2: Travel tips for all the people that love Instagram as a communication instrument.
After you decided your niche, try to check your potential competitors.

Check your potential competitors.

Go inside the "traveleurope" hashtag page and look at the content and potential competitors. To do this, pick a few pictures that you think could compete with your content. You need to visit their profiles.

What kind of picture and video do you see? What kind of capture (Instagram photo description) your competitors use? What kind of hashtags do they use? Observe and note some of the things that you like. **Think about how you can improve the content of your potential competitors.**

Now, look at the list of related hashtags that Instagram offers on top of the page: "travelling_europe", "Europe_ig", etc. Go inside related hashtag posts and look for potential competitors.

Take all your time to study and look at **the related hashtag section as well.**

The related hashtags method is described in the previous chapter.

☐
Chapter 6: How to develop my Instagram social strategy?

In this chapter, you will learn what kind of elements you should research on Instagram to set up your Strategy. When you start with your Instagram account, you must be able to answer the following questions:

How many times per day you have to post?
At what time you have to post?
What kind of content you have to prepare: post, stories, lives?
What kind of hashtags you are going to use?

Instagram research should be one of the first things to do when you'll develop a social strategy.
Focus your attention on the following six types of researches.

1. Research your target if you have already an Instagram account with more than 100 followers.

Now that you decided your potential buyer persona, you should determine how it compares to the demographic characteristics of your actual Instagram followers.
To do this, you should go to your **Instagram Insights** panel and enter the Audience tab.
There can see the age, gender, and location of your followers – three important Instagram metrics that can help you target your future marketing campaigns.

Ideally, this information should provide at least a partial match for your buyer persona. Since you're selling men's luxury watches, your followers should be predominantly men. If Instagram shows that most of your followers are 35-something women, you may need to rethink your current strategy.

To access your Instagram Insights, you'll have to turn your current profile to a business Instagram account, start by logging in, and then follow the steps below.

Go to your profile and tap the "**three lines**" at the top right of your profile.

Step 1: Tap the "three lines"

Step 2: Tap the gear icon for "Settings."

Step 1 and 2.

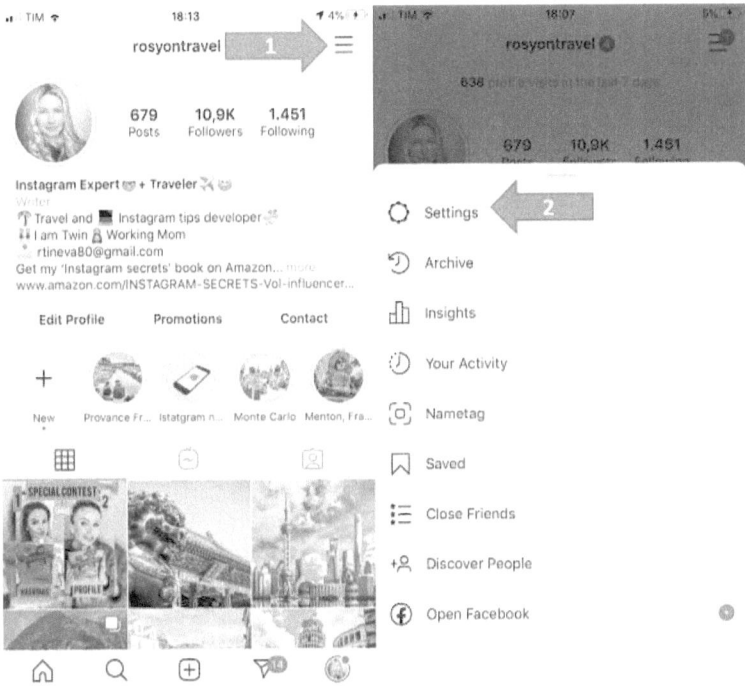

Step 3: Next, hit "Account."

Step 4: Then hit "Switch to Business Profile."

Step 3 and 4

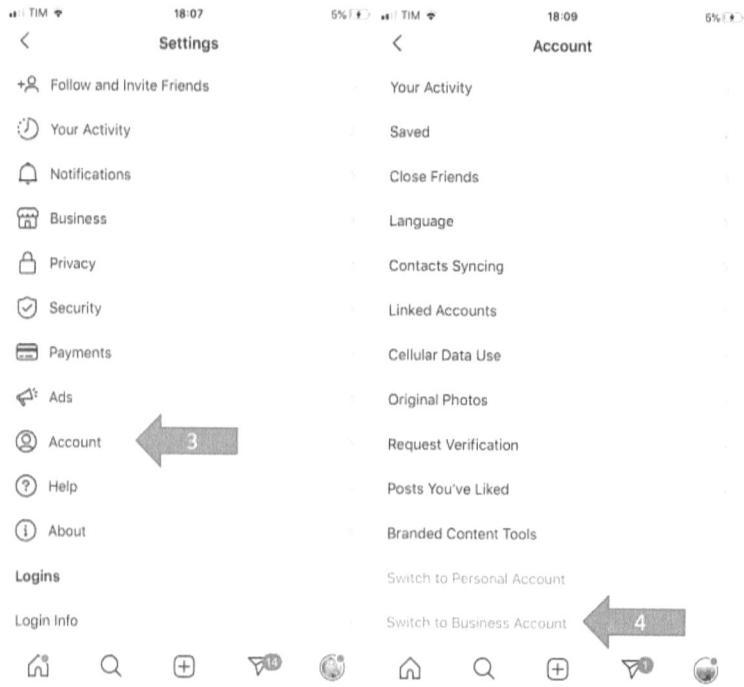

Step 5: Connect to your business Facebook profile if you have one, and add additional business details as directed by Instagram.

Step 5: Tap "Done."

Step 6: After that, you can consult the "Insight" section.

Step 7: Under the "Insights" section, go to "Audience".

In "Audience" you can see some vital statistics about your existing followers including their age range, gender, and location. You can follow the indications described in the next image "How to find the Audience section?"

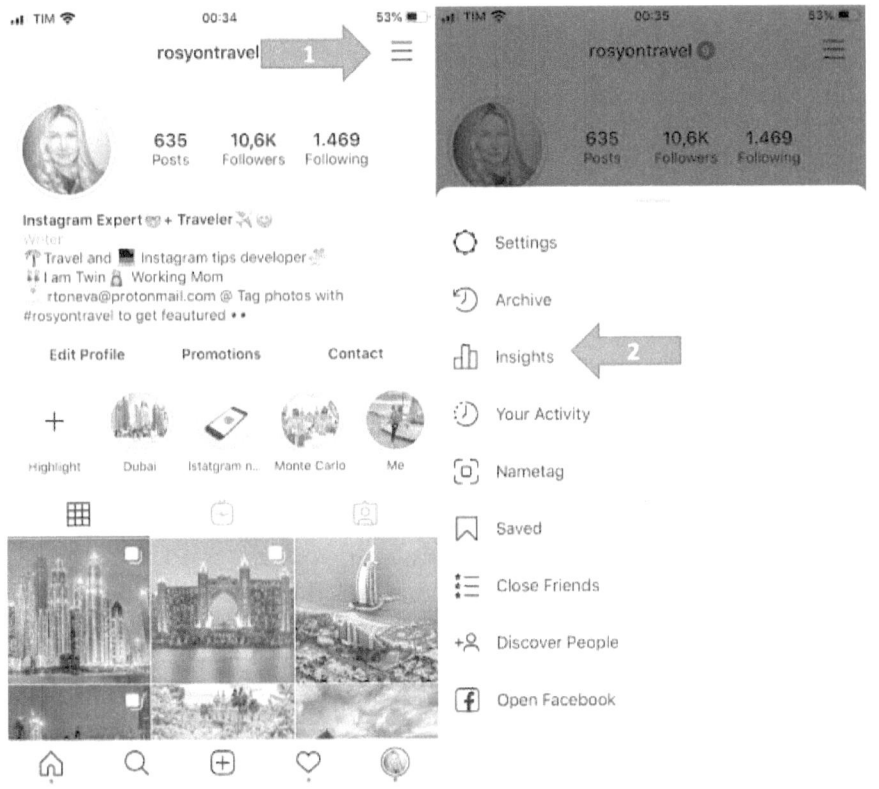

In "Audience section" is where you're able to get a better understanding of who your followers are and where they live, as well as see how your follower number has varied from the previous week.

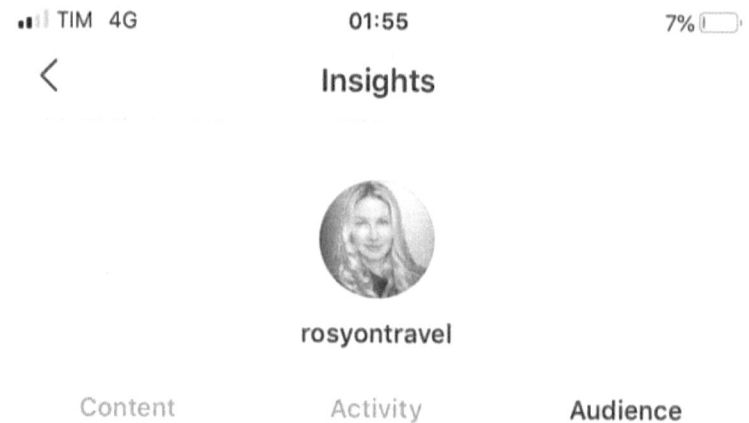

rosyontravel

Content   Activity   **Audience**

Combine this data with your buyer personas and the information you collected from competitor research. This should help you paint a clear picture of what your Instagram target audience looks like. Remember that you can check your "Audience Insight section" only if you have more than 100 followers.

For further information on how to use Instagram Metrics, I invite you to consult my book: Instagram Secrets Vol 6: HOW to use Instagram METRICS. Become an influencer and build a business with no money on Instagram.

2. Find your best time to post.

The "Audience section" that you find in Insights reveals key information about your followers, which can help build and improve your Instagram Marketing Strategy. Not only can you get a better understanding of who follows you, but you can also decipher the time in which your followers are most active, helping you better plan and schedule your Instagram posts to reach the possible people. You can find the following graphic below in your "Audience section". Here you can find a lot of information as to which days your followers are more active and in which time zone.

The image on the next page illustrates what kind of information you can find in the "Audience" section of Instagram Insights.

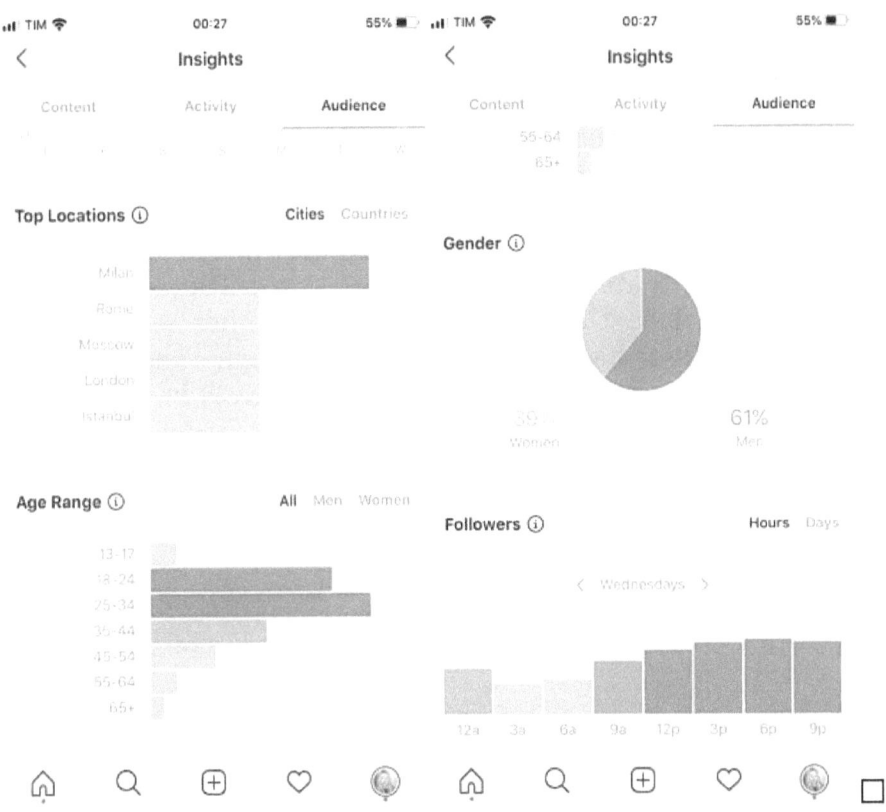

For further information on how to use Instagram Metrics, I invite you to consult my book: Instagram Secrets Vol 6: HOW to use Instagram METRICS. Become an influencer and build a business with no money on Instagram.

3. Research the Interests of your followers.

Once you have a better idea of who your followers are, you also need to research their interests.

To do this, you will need to visit their profiles. Pick a few of your followers who have liked or commented on one of your posts and see what type of content they share on their profiles. Read a few of their captions to get a better sense of the language they use to communicate their ideas. This is important because they may find your content more relatable if you write captions in a style that's similar to their own.

While you're on their profile, click to see what other pages they are following. Although this may take some time, it will give you a better idea of what your followers are looking for on Instagram. During your research, you may notice that many of your followers are interested in, say, cars. They may follow accounts that post car photos or videos. Either way, you can use this information to your advantage and perhaps incorporate a car picture (or any other interest) in one of your future posts.

Other tips are to use Instagram Polls to do your user research. Ask questions, just like you do with the Call to Action in your captions. Ask what topics they're interested in. Ask what format they find more engaging.

Look at the picture on the next page.

4. Research and Collect competitive insight.

If you know your competitors. You can learn a lot about your target audience by looking into your competitors' Instagram audience.

See what kind of followers they have and what kind of posts they are publishing. This can give you some idea of what your Instagram target audience should look like. You can figure out if there are gaps or missing audience segments you've left out as you've started putting together a picture of your audience.

5. Research and Use hashtags in every post.

Instagram's most prominent way to target audiences is through hashtags, as this is how you can reach new audience members and start growing your audience fast.

Using the right Instagram hashtags can dramatically increase your reach on the platform.

However, a lot of people use hashtags passively, that is: they research them, post them, and hope for the best.

Thing is, a target hashtag is the type of hashtag your audience would use on Instagram themselves, so it only makes sense to be proactive. Your target audience should have the same interests as you, so if you use and follow the same hashtags, that's a clear indication you're a good match!

To get further information on how to use Hashtags consult the following my book:

Instagram Secrets Vol 5: HOW to use Instagram HASHTAGS. Become an influencer and build a business with no money on Instagram.

6. Research and write quality captions.

However, there is another verbal element that comes into play when it comes to creating an impact through your captions and writing – and this is by having words in your captions that resonate with your audience. You do not want to be using words that do not make sense to your audience or that sound completely irrelevant or outdated, as this will lead to your audience becoming disinterested in reading what you have to say and struggling to actually "follow" what you are trying to tell them.

The best way to speak like your audience is to pay attention to what they care about by following them back and listening to how they are speaking.

Regularly scroll through your feed and read what the people you follow are saying so that you can get a feel for what their language is like, how they tone their messages, and if there are any unique slang words, phrases, or acronyms that they are using to connect with their audiences. The more you read your niche's captions and comments, the more you are going to become familiar with how they are speaking, what they are saying, and what they are reading. This way, you can begin emulating their language through your posts and saying things in a way that makes sense to your audience.

When you do start emulating your audience, there are a few things that you will need to refrain from doing to avoid having your audience tune out from what you are saying.

 You need to avoid doing is creating messages that are filled with industry jargon that your general following is unlikely to understand.

 If you attempt to use industry jargon that is commonly used between those who sell products and services in the industry, but that is unlikely to be recognizable by those who purchase in or follow the industry, you may lose your following solely because they do not understand you. You do not want to be creating gaps and confusion in your marketing by using language that your audience does not understand because this can make it unnecessarily challenging for people to follow you and support your business.

Keep it simple, speak in a way that your audience will understand, and adapt the industry language to suit your brand's message and purpose. Think always to an exact keyword to create the right call of action.

The next chapter is going to offer you some important tips to follow when you set up your Instagram strategy.

To get further information on how to create Killer consult my book: Instagram Secrets Vol 3: HOW to CREATE Instagram KILLER CONTENTS. Become an influencer and build a business with no money on Instagram.

Chapter 7: The best five tips to grow your Instagram Audience.

In this chapter, you can find some tips that could help you to grow your Audience and Engagement.

1. <u>Saying the Right Thing at the Right Time.</u>

On Instagram, you need to make sure that you are communicating the right thing at the right time. By posting the right content at the right time, you can ensure that you stay relevant and that your content relates to what your audience is going through or thinking about so that your audience will be likely to pay attention to and engage with your content. The easiest way to say the right thing at the right time on Instagram is by following your audience and paying attention to the latest trends, concerns, and issues that may be arising that people are paying attention to.

For instance, if you are in the blogging industry and you blog about current events about famous people, you would want to be staying up-to-date on all of the latest trends and gossip and blogging on them as soon as they reach your eyes. The same would go for any industry you are in. The moment you see a trend or topic waving through your industry, you need to be prepared to get on board with it, customize how you share it according to your unique brand, and offering it as soon as possible.

In addition to following unexpected trends that arise in your industry, you also need to be following expected trends like holidays or scheduled events that are relevant to your audience. For example, if you are in the fashion industry, you should be paying attention to popular fashion events like Fashion Week and the Victoria Secret Fashion Show. If you are in the tech industry, you should be paying attention to the latest device launches and information regarding events that are big in the tech industry, like the annual E3 event. These types of events occur consistently, and they are extremely helpful in allowing you to stay relevant in your industry by paying attention to the information being released by those who drive the industry like influencers and developers.

It is important that you avoid talking about things out of season or out of turn, as sharing information too long after the event occurred can result in you coming across as irrelevant or outdated. Typically, people who see companies sharing outdated information will believe that this company is not paying attention or does not care enough to stay in the loop with what is going on in their industry. As a result, people simply will not follow you.

Remember, we live in the digital age where information can become available fast, and trends can rise and fall even faster. You need to be ready to get into these trends and start creating your brand's name in the heat of the moment and not after the trend or information has already started declining in popularity. If you find that staying on-trend is harder than it looks, try finding three to four people or blogs to follow who are always quick to jump into new trends and solely pay attention to these individuals or resources. This way, you are not overwhelming yourself by trying to follow too many people at once and becoming lost in what is relevant, what is a trend, and what is completely irrelevant to you and your audience.

The content is a King so try to consult my book:

Instagram Secrets Vol 3: HOW to CREATE Instagram KILLER CONTENTS. Become an influencer and build a business with no money on Instagram on Instagram.

2. Use DM (Direct Messaging).

There's nothing wrong with sending a DM to a new follower to ask why they decided to follow you and what is it that they expect to see on your account.

Especially if you notice that someone likes your content regularly or, even better, comments on your stuff all the time. So just slide into their DMs with a casual message!

Here's a simple example that you can use: "Hey! We've noticed you've been following us for a while, thanks so much for the love! Quick question: what kind of content would you like to see us post? We're trying to deliver the best XYZ to our followers, and your feedback would be much appreciated!"

You can consult my book:

Instagram Secrets Vol 7: HOW to use Instagram DIRECT Messaging. Become an influencer and build a business with no money on Instagram.

3. See what's been working, and replicate the success.

If you've been posting for a while, you should start backtracking the engagement rates of your posts to understand what kind of content your audience finds most interesting — and replicate that content in the future.

It's those who are genuinely interested in your content and are eager to interact that are your ideal Instagram audience — and the goal is to find that similar, lookalike audience by posting the type of posts that have proven to be successful before.

4. Use location tagging

For location-based Instagram targeting, you can make the most of the platform's location tagging feature. As location-tagged posts and Stories show up in relevant searches, this feature can significantly enhance your post visibility with the right audience.

5. <u>Connect with the right influencers.</u>

Influencers have authority in specific niches as a direct result of their passion and expertise. They have amassed hundreds of thousands of followers whose interests align with their niche.

So partnering with the right influencers can be highly effective for reaching your Instagram target audience. This would involve a partnership with influencers that your target audience follows and looks up to.

Consult my book for further information:

Instagram Secrets Vol 10: HOW to use Instagram INFLUENCERS. Become an influencer and build a business with no money on Instagram.

The next chapter is going to illustrate one of my methods to increase Instagram followers faster.

Chapter 8: Four-step method to quickly gain Instagram followers.

One of the most important things that any Instagram user wants to know is how to grow quickly his account. Note that start to grow your account is simple, but it is important to create a quality community and you can do this only if you read all my books. Do not stop here in your learning process. Let's start with my method.

Step 1: Consistently post feeds and Instagram stories. At least one post per day and at least 3 stories per day. Try to change the content of the feed: once you can post a city image, once you can post a portrait. Instagram likes a variety of pictures.

You can find further information on how to create Killer contents in my book: Instagram Secrets Vol 3: HOW to CREATE Instagram KILLER CONTENTS, Become an influencer, and build a business with no money on Instagram.

Step 2: Insert 30 relevant Hashtags in each post. Hashtags are very important to increase your post impressions. You have to learn how to use better this tool.

You can find further information on how to use Hashtags in my book. Instagram Secrets Vol 5: HOW to use Instagram HASHTAGS. Become an influencer and build a business with no money on Instagram.

Step 3: Start to use the follow/ unfollow technique. Follow some big target accounts and then unfollow them.

The Follow/ Unfollow is an Instagram growth technique. You need to identify some big target accounts which have followers that might be interested in your profile and start following them. That's a quick and fast technique to gain immediately some followers and particularly recommended for personal and brand accounts in the startup stage.

I would like to give you some practical examples.

In this stage, you are going to apply the logic of a differentiated portfolio that the financial experts use in their daily work.

You need to find 5 different clusters of big Instagram accounts with over 1 million followers.

Take as an example "Instagram Travel account for Moms".

The clusters could be the following: Travel, Photography; Instagram Famous accounts, Animals, Influencers Mom, Here the list of accounts that I have selected as an example.

-        10 accounts that speak about **Travel** with over 1 million followers:

#tripadvisor – 2.4 M
#easrth – 1.1 M
#beautifulhotels – 3.3 M
#natgeoadventure – 5.9 M
#natgeowild – 8.3 M
#travelandleisure – 4.8M
#gopro -16.6 M
#natgeotravel – 35.7M
#natgeoimagecollection – 11.9M
#traveler – 2.4 M

- 10 account of **Photography** or photographers that have over 1 million followers:

#chrisburkard – 3.5 M
#danielkordan – 1.2 M
#canon_photos – 2.9 M
#artofvisual – 1.9 M
#clarklittle – 2.2 M
#ladzinski – 1.6 M
#maxrivephotography – 1.7M
#surfline – 1.7M

#jimmychin – 2.5 M

-       10 accounts of **Very famous people on Instagram** that have over 20 million followers:
#cristiano – 193M
#camila_cabello – 45.10 M
#davidbeckham – 59.8M
#selenagomez – 164 M
#taylorswift – 124 M
#arianagrande – 169 M
#kourtneykardash – 84.4 M
#mileycyrus- 102M

10 **Accounts of animal lovers** with over 1 million followers:
#animalplanet – 3.1M
#world_wildlife – 3.2 M
#disney – 22.1 M
#natgeochannel – 4.4 M
#greenpeace – 2.9 M
#discovery.hd – 1.7 M
#amivitale – 1.1 M
#thedodo – 7.7M
#discoverocean- 2.4M

-       10 accounts of "**Influencer Mom with child**" with over 1 million followers.
#melitatoniolo
#alicecampello
#diaryofafitmommyofficial
#khloekardashian
#kayla_itsines
#womenshealthmag
#kourtneykardash
#kristenanniebell
#jennifer.garner
#jessicaalba

To find these accounts you can use the option "suggested by Instagram". If you do not remember how to find "Suggested by Instagram "accounts, check the paragraph: **How to find similar accounts "Suggested by Instagram"?**

It is recommended to have an idea for at least one account of each category illustrated above and then you can use the "Suggested by Instagram" tool.

To be easier to follow and unfollow the accounts that you found it is better to search for Instagram verified badge accounts – accounts with blue tick as illustrated below.

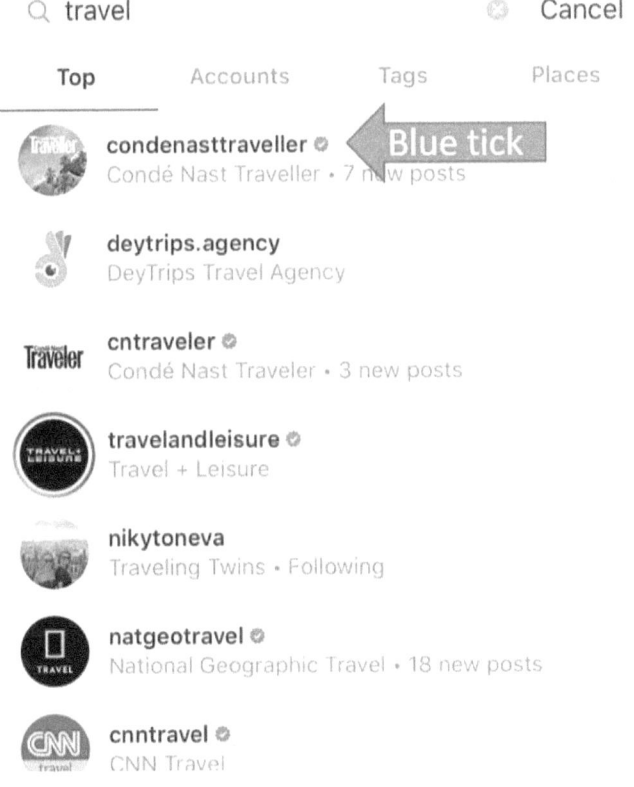

Now start to follow and unfollow all the accounts that you have identified above.

You have to do these two operations (follow and unfollow) every single day. At least 4 times per day (at 10 am; 2 pm; 6 pm; 11.00 pm) you have to make one operation of follow 40 accounts and unfollow 40 accounts at 10 am, then another operation of following 40 accounts and unfollowing 40 accounts at 1 pm and so on.

Note that there's nothing wrong with sending a DM to each new follower to introduce yourself and the service that you are offering. You can send standard messages as follow:

"Hey! I've noticed you've been following me for a while, thanks so much for your follow!" Insert a quick presentation of what kind of content your followers could find in your account and why you must follow you.

I would like to give you another example to help you to clarify the method illustrated above using a small local business.
Take this example, a small local beauty center in Los Angelis.
1) Find Instagram accounts of Local TV, newspapers, radio show, or magazines. Follow and unfollow them.
2) Find Instagram accounts of local stars or politics. Follow and unfollow them.
3) Find Instagram accounts of a famous local bar, restaurants.
4) Find Instagram accounts of local famous beauty bloggers.
5) Find your Instagram competitors and follow them.
6) Try to create a relationship with the followers of your direct competitors. Put likes, comment on their posts, and follow them.
7) Use the keyword "beauty center" in the tags section and select some of the hashtags that Instagram shows you. Try to comment on the picture that you see with relevant ideas or suggestions.

Step 4: Use Engagement to get more followers on Instagram.
You have to learn how to find and engage with real people. Think that you need engaging followers not just followers.

The best way to find real followers is to go out and engage with them on their profiles in meaningful ways.

What is a "**meaningful** "form of engagement in the eyes of the Instagram algorithm?

The meaningful comment is at least **4 words** long and not repeated a lot of time from the same user across different pictures and posts. Think that if you receive like from one account is cool, but if you get a comment you are a little bit happier and potentially you can check out the profile. The comments are more meaningful then likes but it is important to get a comment from somebody that is going to catch your attention. The worst thing that you can do is to leave the same comments as "nice picture", "great post" .this comments could be considered spammy.

My recommendation is to look at the caption of the post. Read it and try to make a follow-up question and try to inspire the person to answer you and to start a real conversation and connection. You have to think to find individually your followers as the door to door marketing.

Where you can find ideal potential followers? I would like to list five places where you can find your ideal follower:

I)   **Location tags or hashtags** – this is the perfect place if you have a local business account. In this way, you can find people in your area. You can use the location tag even you have a personal account.

II)   **IIashtags tags.** This is the perfect tool if you have a niche account. My recommendation is to find hashtags relevant to your topic that you are posted about. Try to say something meaningful to them with your comments. It is very important, as discussed in the first three chapters, to find your target audience and after that try to reach it.

III) **Leave comments on the post of industry leaders** in your niche. Leave value comments or answers. These people have a big potential to leverage their audience. You can find the best industry leaders for your account following the method "**How to find competitor's accounts?" described in chapter 4 of this book.**

IV) **Tag the photos of industry leaders' accounts if the picture is relevant to your content.**

V) **Like or comment on the picture of your followers.** It is highly possible that the people that follow you have friends that potentially could be interested in your account as well.

I would like to give you some practical example of how to find hashtag or location tag:

- Tap Instagram magnifying glass;

- Find the "Search section", write the keyword "Travel" into the search bar.

- Click on the "Tag" or "Location" tab.

- You can choose one of the "hashtags" listed in the travel section on Instagram

- Then click on the "Recent" section.

- You can try to comment on at least 90 of the most recent photos. Try to make useful and relevant comments on the posts. You can try to split the comments of the 90 photos into 3 sessions, that is, a session of 30 comments in the morning, one of 30 comments of lunch, and one of 30 comments in the evening.

I would like to share with you my Instagram engagement routine as well.

1) Replay every single comment in the first 30 min. Try to start a conversation.
2) Say hello to every single new follower.
3) Reach out to who you follow. Send DM messages to people that you follow. In this way, you can start networking with the accounts you admire.
4) Leave comments on Industry Leader' pictures in your niche that have a similar demographic target as you. Sometimes the big accounts do not have time to answer all questions that the people ask, so you can use this opportunity and answer questions that remain without any answer.
5) Check accounts that comment on your last picture, and go to their accounts, try to like the last 9 pictures, and comment on one of their pictures.

Try to apply the four-step for 2 weeks, after you are going to get more than 100 followers to try to check your "Insights" section and to define your "Instagram Audience".

Keep in mind that you can check your "Instagram Insights" only 1 week after you got a business profile. And only after you have at least 100 followers. So, it is very important to generate followers in this first period to find your Instagram target.

Note that the Instagram algorithm has limits that you have to respect. Otherwise, your account could be blocked. I am going to give you further details about this method in my book: Instagram Secrets Vol 4: HOW to OUTSMART Instagram ALGORITHM. Become an influencer and build a business with no money on Instagram.

Chapter 9: Homework Section

This chapter is for people who want to practice Self-reflection. Self-reflection is the habit of paying attention to your thoughts and decisions. I would like to guide your thinking process with some questions. I have created question sections according to what kind of account do you have:
- An influencer with a new Instagram account or existing account with less than 100 followers.
- An influencer with an already existing Instagram account and over 100 followers.
- Small business with a new Instagram account or existing account with less than 100 followers.
- Small business with already existing accounts and over 100 followers.

Try to understand which of the four categories listed above fit better with your account, and answer some of the questions.
Let's start with the first category.

An influencer with a new Instagram account or existing account with less than 100 followers

1.   Think about some activities that you love to do? List all of them below.
Ex: travel, sport, fitness, art, cooking
2.   Think about 5 problems or needs that you faced in the past related to some of the activities listed above?
....
3.   Could you offer some solutions to the problems indicated above?
....
4.   Are you able to maintain your idea for a long time as content?
....
5.   Could this solution generate income?

....

6.   How do you think to generate Incomes?

....

7.   Do your target clients are Millennials?

....

If the answer is, yes to all three last questions above. You can create an Instagram page around the problem that you have found.

8.   Think about the exact target audience. Who is your audience: (age, gender, location, income level, level of education, interests, and lifestyle)?

Create 3 different profiles and give a name to all of them.

Profile 1.......

Profile 2 ......

Profile 3......

Each profile has to include the following information, use Profile 1 as an example.

Profile 1:

Age: 25 – 32

Gender: Female

Location: Urban

Income Level: $35 000 – $47.000

Level of Education: College Graduate

Interests: reading business books; pinning healthy eating recipes.

Hobbies: yoga or running.

Challenges: what kind of new content you can provide to this specific profile? How you can impress this segment?

Goals: Create goals that your target audience wants to engage with. What kind of engage rate do you want to reach in 1 month?

You have to do this work for each profile: 2, 3, 4, etc.

You should always think about what your audience expects to see on your profile.

Next, you'll focus on their hobbies and interests as well as the challenges and goals they face. Hobbies and interests will play an essential role in identifying who follow your Instagram page. Think that your target audience can help you identify what sorts of topics to cover.

9.   Check how popular is your Idea on Instagram, to know how big could be potentially your account. Use chapter 5 of this book, paragraph: *"Check how popular your niche in Instagram is?"*

10.   Try to apply a 3-step level down the formula. Use chapter 5 of this book, paragraph: *"3-step level down" formula for finding a niche"*.

11.   Try to check your potential competitor's profiles? Check chapter 5 of this book, paragraph: *"How to find my potential competitors"*.

12.   Generate followers as indicated in chapter 8.

13.   After you get 100 followers try to turn your Instagram profile into a business to check the Insights. Check chapter 6: *"Research your target if you have already an Instagram account with more than 100 followers."*

An influencer with an already existing account and more than 100 followers.

1. Turn your profile in the Business or Creator profile. Check chapter 6 of this book, paragraph: *"Research your target if you have already an Instagram account with more than 100 followers".*

2. Check the section "Audience" of Insights. Try to research your followers are in line with your audience strategy.

3. Check 100 random profiles of your followers. Research which is the Interest of your followers. Try to understand:

-   What kind of feeds do they post?
-   What kind of account do they follow?
-   What kind of language do they use in the capture space?

4. Find your competitors If you are not aware. Think about 5 relevant keywords that describe better your project. Insert these words into the Instagram search bar. Check what kind of accounts Instagram offers you and visit them. Check chapter 5 of this book, paragraph: *"How to find my potential competitors".*

5. Check your competitor's accounts, visit their profiles, and answer the following questions:
-   What kind of content do they post?
-   How many times?
-   What kind of hashtags?
-   What kind of caption?
Think about how you can improve all of the elements above.

6. Generate followers as indicated in chapter 8.

A small business without an Instagram account or with an Instagram account with less than 100 followers.

1. Think about what kind of customers you have? What are your target market and audience? Follow what is illustrated in Chapter 3: "Should I use Instagram as a Target Audience tool?"

2. Think about the exact target audience. Who is your audience: (age, gender, location, income level, level of education, interests, and lifestyle)?

Create 3 different profiles and give a name to all of them.
Profile 1.......
Profile 2 ......
Profile 3......

Each profile has to include the following information, use Profile 1 as an example.

Profile 1:

Age: 25 – 32

Gender: Female

Location: Urban

Income Level: $35 000 – $47.000

Level of Education: College Graduate

Interests: reading business books; pinning healthy eating recipes.

Hobbies: yoga or running.

Challenges: what kind of new content you can provide to this specific profile? How you can impress this segment?

Goals: Create goals that your target audience wants to engage with. What kind of engage rate do you want to reach in 1 month?

You have to do this work for each profile: 2, 3, 4, etc.

You should always think about what your audience expects to see on your profile.

Next, you'll focus on their hobbies and interests as well as the challenges and goals they face. Hobbies and interests will play an essential role in identifying who follow your Instagram page. Think that your target audience can help you identify what sorts of topics to cover.

3. Think about your Target audience? Do your Target audience are Millennials? If the answer is yes. You can think to invest your time to build an Instagram account and brand.

4. Think about your direct competitors? Do you know the name of your competitors? If yes, check if they have an Instagram profile and what kind of content and hashtag they use. Check how many times they post in 1 week. Try to think about how to set up your strategy and to improve competitor's ones as well.

4. Find your competitors If you are not aware. Think about 5 relevant keywords that describe better your project. Insert these words into the Instagram search bar. Check what kind of accounts Instagram offers you. Use the paragraph: *"Check your potential competitors"*.

5. Generate followers as indicated in Chapter 8.

6. Turn your Instagram profile in business to check the Insights. Check chapter 6: *"Research your target if you have already an Instagram account with more than 100 followers."*

Small Business Account that already has an Instagram page and over 100 followers.

1.   Turn your profile in the Business or Creator profile. Check chapter 6 of this book, paragraph: *"Research your target if you have already an Instagram account with more than 100 followers"*.

2.   Check the section *"Audience"* of Insights. Try to check if your account followers are in line with your audience strategy. For example, if you have a restaurant in Milano and you find that the bigger part of your followers are from the USA you have to adjust urgently your Instagram strategy. In the "Audience "section you are going to find a lot of information about your followers.

3.   Check 100 random profiles of your followers. Try to understand:

-       What kind of feeds do they post?
-       What kind of account do they follow?
-       What kind of language do they use in the capture space?

4.   Check the profile of your direct competitors. If you aware of your Instagram competitors or account with similar contents as yours try to check:

-       What kind of content do they post?
-       How many times?
-       What kind of hashtags?
-       What kind of caption?
Think about how you can improve all of the elements above.

5.   Find your competitors. If you are not aware of your competitors. Think about 5 relevant keywords that describe better your project. Insert these words into an Instagram search bar. Check what kind of accounts Instagram offers you. Check chapter 5 of this book, paragraph: *"How to find my potential competitors"*.

6.   Generate new followers to improve your Instagram Audience as indicated in chapter 8.

7.   Turn your Instagram profile in business to check the Insights. Check chapter 6: *"Research your target if you have already an Instagram account with more than 100 followers."*

Conclusions

Congratulation that you finish one of the 12 books: **Instagram Secrets Vol 1: HOW to find the right Instagram AUDIENCE**. Become an influencer and build a business with no money on Instagram.

Defining the target audience is the primary task every marketer has to take on to develop an effective Instagram growth strategy. Before you present yourself or your brand in any way, you need to know exactly who you do it for.

What's their age, gender, interests? What content do they consider great? Once you answer these and determine your audience, you will need to figure out how to find it on Instagram, engage, and grow.

Researching your ideal target audience on Instagram is not a one-time project. There's no way to figure this out one time and go straight into content creation and promotion and never have to worry about it again.

Instagram target audience research is a work in progress. The more time you take, the more you learn about your audience — and then ultimately, the more refined and targeted your content strategy becomes.

☐

Other books

I hope that this book added value and quality to your social knowledge. If you enjoyed this book and found some benefit in reading this, I'd like to inform you that you can find in the Kindle store (Amazon) the following short guides that make part of the serial set.

Instagram Secrets Vol 1: HOW to find the right Instagram AUDIENCE. Become an influencer and build a business with no money on Instagram. (Short social media marketing book).

Instagram Secrets Vol 2: HOW to Build the Perfect Instagram Profile. Become an influencer and build a business with no money on Instagram. (Short social media marketing book).

Instagram Secrets Vol 3: HOW to CREATE Instagram KILLER CONTENTS. Become an influencer and build a business with no money on Instagram. (Short social media marketing book).

Instagram Secrets Vol 4 HOW to OUTSMART Instagram ALGORITHM. Become an influencer and build a business with no money on Instagram. (Short social media marketing book).

Instagram Secrets Vol 5: HOW to use Instagram HASHTAGS. Become an influencer and build a business with no money on Instagram. (Short social media marketing book).

Instagram Secrets Vol 6: HOW to use Instagram METRICS. Become an influencer and build a business with no money. (Short social media marketing book).

Instagram Secrets Vol 7: HOW to use Instagram DIRECT Messaging, Become an influencer, and build a business with no money on Instagram. (Short social media marketing book).

Instagram Secrets Vol 8: HOW to use Instagram IGTV content. Become an influencer and build a business with no money on Instagram. (Short social media marketing book).

Instagram Secrets Vol 9: HOW to use Instagram CONTESTS. Become an influencer and build a business with no money on Instagram. (Short social media marketing book).

Instagram Secrets Vol 10: HOW to use Instagram INFLUENCERS. Become an influencer and build a business with no money on Instagram. (Short social media marketing book).

Instagram Secrcts Vol 11: HOW to use Instagram AUTOMATION TOOLS. Become an influencer and build a business with no money on Instagram. (Short social media marketing book)

Instagram Secrets Vol 12: How to generate PROFITS from Instagram. Become an influencer and build a business with no money on Instagram. (Short social media marketing book).

Do not forget about my special Bonus. Get one of my books for free just by sending me your email at rtineva80@gmail.com

If you want to know more about how to find the best-related accounts for your profile, I'll recommend you to contact me personally and to get my private lessons. In one hour, I am going to explain to you better the method below.

About the author

Hello, nice to meet you in this virtual space. Now it's time to introduce myself.

My name is Rosy Toneva, and I am a Commercial and Marketing B2B expert for some of the largest European Airlines. I enjoy traveling, writing, snapping pictures. I spend time daily writing and updating my Instagram blog @rosyontravel. I believe in one religion - Traveling!

I love educating and inspiring other people to succeed and live the life of their dream. I often repeat myself: If more than 50% of my brain believes it, it will come true.

I think that social media allows people to interact with others and offer multiple ways for marketers to reach and engage with consumers.

Now I would like to share with you how I started this project.

In April 2019, I decided to test my Instagram profile. I wanted to grow my Instagram account through my two passions, "Travel and Marketing". At the time, my account @rosyontravel had around 560 followers. I wanted to increase my followers in an organic way (no buying fake followers), no huge investing. I just desired to see what I could do by putting forth a conscious effort as a normal person did. It's been an intense four-month experiment of seeing what works and what doesn't. After only four months, I gained 10k loyal followers. Thanks to a lot of tests I prepared a set of twelve books, named Instagram secrets that you can find on Amazon. The advantage of these books is that they are very simple and do not offer trivial tips. The good news is that I am a normal person like you so you can just check my page and say hello.

You can follow my Instagram profile (@rosyontravel) to get further information and updated news about Instagram.

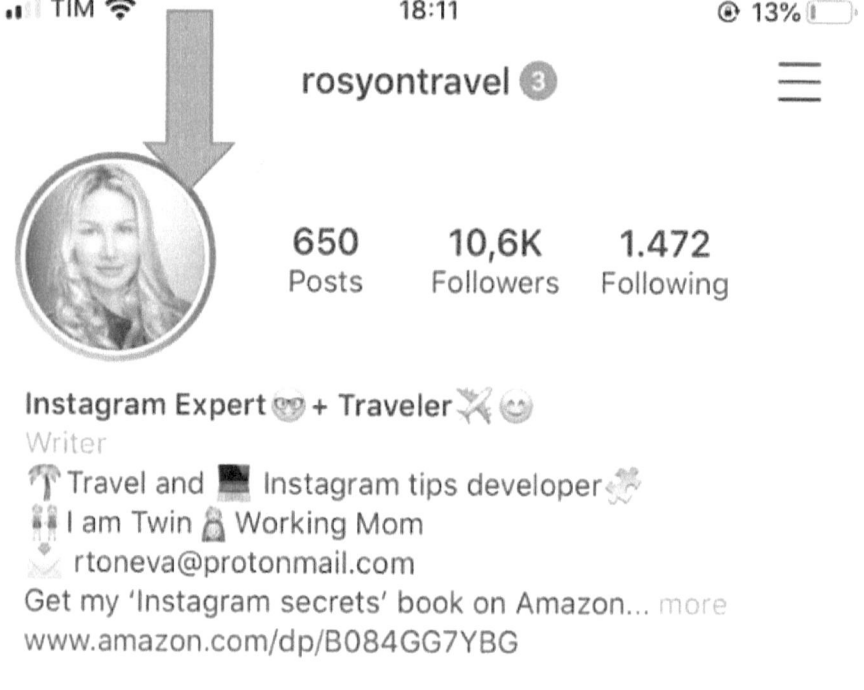

If you want to know more about Instagram secrets methods described in this book, please contact me personally. Send an email to rtineva8o@gmail.com or use Instagram Direct messaging.

One last thing

If you enjoyed this book and found some benefit in reading this, I'd like to hear from you and hope that you could take some time to post a review on Amazon. Your feedback and support will help me to greatly improve my writing craft for future projects and make this book even better.

Thank you and I wish you all the best in your future success.

Common Instagram terms you should know

Bio - This is the biography of your profile on Instagram. This is your place to tell the world a little bit about yourself. You can use text, emojis, hashtags, and even '@' mention profiles here.

Mention - This is how you get someone's attention on Instagram. Begin with the @ symbol, followed by their handle or name. If you're following them, you'll find their handle in the first couple of autocomplete options. You can mention someone in a variety of places on Instagram, including in your bio, comments, or even in Instagram Stories.

Tag - Tag is different from Mention. You can only tag a person on a picture or a video. When you tag someone, it will show up in their profile (in the tagged section next to their Gallery).

Instagram Algorithm – An algorithm is a detailed step-by-step instruction set or formula for solving a problem or completing a task. In computing, programmers write algorithms that instruct the computer how to perform a task. Instagram Algorithm is several rules that the application follows to protect her community from spamming users and to set up the company earning a strategy.

Instagram Bots – These are automated profiles masquerading as people. But sometimes, even legit profiles use automated bots (third-party services) to get your attention. If you come across random comments on your posts or a slew of likes seconds after you post a picture, a bot was probably involved in the process.

Business Profile - Instagram offers a simple way to switch from a personal profile to a business profile. You don't even need to be a registered business to use a business profile. And there are many advantages to converting to a business profile. You get access to action buttons in the bio and you get detailed insights from your followers. Plus, using a business profile is the only way to unlock features like embedding links in Stories and adding buy buttons to your posts.

Insights - Once you've converted to a Business Profile, you'll see an Insights button in the top toolbar in your profile. Tap on it and you'll find a sea of useful information. You'll find out what the age and gender breakdown of your followers is, as well as the best time to post to Instagram for maximum engagement.

Explore page - Tap on the Search button from the bottom toolbar and you'll end up in the Explore tab. This is the hodgepodge of everything that's trending on Instagram right now. On the top, you'll find topics, and below, a feed of popular photos and videos.

Home page - The Home screen is the list of activities of all the users you follow. Also referred to as the feed.

Swipe up –It is a feature that allows you to add links to your stories. Now, all Instagram business accounts with 10,000 or more followers can add links to Instagram Stories. Up until recently, this feature was only available to verified Instagram accounts (accounts with sign V).

Instagram Direct – Direct is a private messaging feature on Instagram. It allows users to share private messages with one or multiple users in a group.

IGTV - IGTV video is an app that can be used alone or in tandem with Instagram. It's essentially Instagram's answer to YouTube.

Instagram Stories - is a feature within the Instagram app where users can capture and post related images and video content in a slideshow format. In both apps, content is available for only 24 hours from the time of posting. Stories allow the addition of text, drawings, and emoticons to images or video clips.

Instagram contest - is a great way to get more followers, build an engaged audience, and grow your brand. The contest is a promotional scheme in which participants compete for prizes by accomplishing something that requires skill. Although no fee is charged for participating in a contest.

API – The term API is an acronym, and it stands for "Application Programming Interface." The API is not the database or even the server, it is the code that governs the access point(s) for the server. They allow us to go get data from outside sources. To explain this better, let us take a familiar example. Imagine you're sitting at a table in a restaurant with a menu of choices to order from. The kitchen is part of the "system" that will prepare your order. What is missing is the critical link to communicate your order to the kitchen and deliver your food back to your table. That's where the waiter or API comes in. The waiter is the messenger – or API – that takes your request or order and tells the kitchen – the system – what to do. Then the waiter delivers the response back to you; in this case, it is the food.

IP Address - It's a network address for your computer so the Internet knows where to send you emails, data, and pictures.
With this short guide, I'm going to give you a deep dive into how to use Instagram hashtags to increase your followers. Using the right hashtags is fundamental. If you include the right Instagram hashtags on your posts or stories, you will likely see higher engagement than you would if you didn't have any.

Instagram Creator Studio - Instagram creator studio helps Instagram users to manage their Instagram presence much more conveniently. The Creator Studio was only available for Facebook pages earlier, is now available for Instagram business and creator accounts. Note that Creator Studio for both Instagram and Facebook is only available on the desktop now. You can find inside Instagram Creator Studio the following information:
- Detailed growth data and Insights
- Number of daily activities
- Scheduling posts.
- Simplified messaging on Instagram since you have access to all the comments and messages all in one place.
- Use a set of cool soundtracks for Instagram videos for more impressions.

Instagram proxies - a proxy is a server that acts as an intermediary for its user's requests. In the beginning, proxy servers were used only for privacy and anonymity. Instagram proxies are developed to be used by marketers to automate several social media accounts at the same time. There are only a few proxy providers offering Instagram proxies because social networks are some of the most restrictive websites proxies. For Instagram, proxies are used to connect an Instagram account permanently through a single dedicated IP address in this way, one person can control several accounts. And vice-versa, one Instagram profile can be managed by several employees working remotely

VPN - Virtual Private Network, allows you to create a secure connection to another network over the Internet. People get VPNs for "privacy and security".
Are you confused between VPN and Proxies? VPN and proxies both help to keep users anonymous
VPN is almost similar to the Proxies, but its a lot more versatile and most safe. Another best thing about VPN is that it encrypts 100% of your internet traffic and routes it through VPN servers making you entirely anonymous.